I0408924

Discovering Your Financial Success Roadmap

Unlocking the Journey to Financial Bliss

George T.Y

All rights reserved. No part of this publication may be reproduced, distributed, or transmitted in any form or by any means, including photocopying, recording, or other electronic or mechanical methods, without the prior written permission of the publisher, except in the case of brief quotations embodied in critical reviews and certain other noncommercial uses permitted by copyright law.

Copyright © George T.Y, 2023.

Table Of Content

Introduction

Meet Sarah; she's a new grad with big ideas and ambitions. She was ready to rule the world after getting her first job. But as she made her way through the early phases of her profession, she discovered that she was up against a powerful foe: her money.

Like many of us, Sarah had a complicated relationship with money that included both goals and problems. She envisioned a life free from financial stress in which she could follow her interests, protect her future, and make lasting memories with her loved ones. But college debts, credit card debt, and the distant ambition of property appeared to be obstacles in the way of realizing this dream.

Sarah wanted a blueprint, a manual that would show her the path to financial success while she struggled with these issues. She yearned for independence and stability, not just a quick cure, but a long-lasting transformation—a path that would open the door to financial pleasure.

If you can identify with Sarah's experience, if you've ever been financially challenged or have fantasized about attaining genuine financial success, you're not alone. You may use this book, "Discovering Financial Success Roadmap," as a compass when traveling toward financial fulfillment.

You will discover a road map on these pages that is customized to your requirements, goals, and particular situation. Together, we will traverse the personal financial landscape while tackling the obstacles that have prevented you from achieving your goals. This book is for everyone who wants to learn the skill of managing money, whether they are fresh graduates like Sarah, ambitious business owners, parents who want to secure the future of their families, or anybody else.

But this isn't simply another dull financial manual replete with technical terms. It's a transformational experience that mixes a dash of imagination with real-world knowledge. Along the way, you'll discover the actual meaning of financial joy, which is a way of life where money serves as a tool rather than a burden, where your aspirations become attainable objectives, and where the trip itself is just as rewarding as the final destination.

Turn the page now if you're prepared to start on this thrilling journey to financial achievement. Your path to financial fulfillment has just begun.

Hello and thank you for visiting "Discovering Financial Success Roadmap: Unlocking the Journey to Financial Bliss." The desire for financial joy unites us all in the world of personal finance. It's a desire that goes beyond the details of money because it's about acquiring the freedom and security to live life on your terms rather than just amassing a fortune.

This book is your road map for making that desire a practical reality as well as your trusty friend and guide. You, the reader, a varied and dynamic population of people with particular needs, goals, pain spots, and wants, are the target audience for it.

You may be a fresh graduate entering the financial industry who is looking to grasp the complexities of budgeting and investing as you hold these pages in your hands. Or maybe you're an entrepreneur who hopes to expand your company and provide for your family. You could be close to retiring, dreaming of a leisurely and fulfilling life, or you might just want to improve your financial literacy and ability to make wise choices.

This book is your key to opening the door to the path to financial joy, regardless of your stage in life or your financial goals. We will go deeply into personal economics and address the issues that often leave us feeling unsettled and overburdened. Together, we'll discover methods for overcoming financial stress, making your money work for you, and securing a future that aligns with your most cherished goals.

However, this book is more than simply a how-to guide for money matters. A path that should be in line with your beliefs, emotions, and aspirations should be taken to achieve financial success, according to this tale. It involves developing a mentality that enables you to make confident and prudent financial decisions, whether you want to escape the chains of debt, succeed in your profession, prepare for a happy retirement, or leave a lasting legacy.

We shall set off on this trip together in the chapters that come after this one. We will go into the complexities of setting a budget, saving money, investing, advancing your career, preparing for retirement, and much more. But keep in mind that the goal here is to achieve financial joy, a condition in which money is used as a tool to support your aspirations and enhance your life, not merely to amass fortune.

So buckle up and get ready to travel your route to financial achievement. The voyage begins here, with financial joy as the final objective. Together, let's go out on this transformational journey and bring your fantasies of financial fulfillment to life.

Chapter 1

Dreaming of Financial Happiness

What does financial joy mean to you? is a question that stands out in the vastness of our financial travels like a compass. When thoughtfully considered, this question exposes the core of your innermost ambitions and objectives. This chapter serves as the beginning point for our joint exploration of the Financial Success Roadmap. This trip starts with comprehending the goal, which is your particular idea of financial fulfillment.

The Influence of Ambition

Being successful financially is a very personal goal. It's not about following societal norms irrationally or adhering to other people's expectations. It is instead important to create a financial strategy that fits your ambitions, beliefs, and objectives. It is building a life where money serves as a tool to help you accomplish what is genuinely important.

It's important to recognize the power of desire before getting into the actual procedures and techniques of managing your money, making sensible investments, and protecting your future. Your financial path might be sparked with purpose and passion by your ambitions and objectives. They serve as the impetus for all of your financial decisions, large or small.

What Is Financial Happiness?

We must first specify our endpoint, which is financial joy, to chart the road towards financial success. Some people define financial joy as reaching a specific amount of money, being able to retire comfortably, or attaining a long-held goal. Others may define it as being debt-free, having the freedom to travel, contributing to their community, or just having financial peace of mind.

We'll take an introspective trip in this chapter to discover your definition of financial joy. We'll prod you with probing inquiries and deep reflection to help you come to a clear understanding of what is most important to you in terms of your financial journey. Through this approach, you'll start to sketch out the general contours of your financial roadmap—a roadmap that isn't standardized but rather uniquely crafted to meet your goals and desires.

Your Journey Begins

It's important to keep in mind that there are no right or incorrect answers as we discuss the complexities of financial joy. Your life experiences, ideals, and objectives have all influenced how you see money. You are not only getting clarity by taking this action, but you are also moving forward toward a time in the future when your financial choices are in line with your aspirations.

In the chapters that follow, we'll provide you with the information, resources, and tactics you need to make your goals a reality. We are here to be your guides as you travel toward financial happiness, assisting you as you negotiate the curves and detours of the Financial Success Roadmap.

So let's start this journey by delving deeply into your financial fantasies and opening the door to your interpretation of financial fulfillment. Together, we will light the way forward and work patiently to realize your goals.

Section 1

Increasing Control and Confidence

Do you ever spend the whole night thinking about your bills, debts, and the never-ending cycle of spending while looking at the ceiling? Or maybe you've experienced that anxiety-inducing twinge every time you check your bank account, wondering whether there will ever be enough money to support your goals and aspirations.

It's not just you.

Welcome to Section 1 of the "Discovering Financial Success Roadmap," where we'll set out on a life-changing adventure to give you back control over your finances and put an end to those restless nights. We'll address one of the most prevalent obstacles to financial success head-on in this section: financial stress.

Stress related to money might seem like an immovable mountain, looming over all facets of your life. It's the constant concern about how you're going to pay your bills, the stress about unplanned crises, and the nagging feeling that you might be doing better. The reality is that you have the strength to climb this mountain.

We'll get deeply into the core of your money concerns in Chapter 2, "Overcoming Money Stress." We'll look at the psychological and emotional components of money that keep you up at night and give you doable solutions to lighten the load. This chapter will provide you with the knowledge and attitude required to take control of your financial future, whether you're battling with growing debts, bleak employment prospects, or just trying to make sense of your money.

You'll have the information and confidence necessary by the conclusion of this chapter to tackle your financial stress head-on and transform it from a crippling force into a catalyst for change. It's time to take the first step toward financial freedom, which starts with overcoming your money worries. Together, let's start along this transforming journey.

Chapter 2

Reducing Financial Stress

Introduction

It's all too easy to become caught in a spiral of financial worry and anxiety in today's fast-paced society. The amount of bills that need to be paid keeps increasing, unanticipated costs keep popping up, and the worry that there won't be enough money may become a constant worry. But do not worry; in this chapter, we will examine the causes of financial stress and provide you with tools to help you restore control over your finances.

Knowing What Causes Financial Stress

Different things might cause financial stress. Increasing credit card debt, job insecurity, or the perception that your financial objectives are slipping more out of reach might all be contributing factors. Recognizing the underlying reasons for this stress is the first step in conquering it. You can start addressing the triggers more successfully if you can pinpoint their precise nature.

The Evil Cycle

Many of us have gone through a stressful financial cycle. Often, it begins with an unanticipated expenditure or a decrease in income, which causes concern and restless nights. This stress may then have a cascading impact on your relationships, general well-being, and even your ability to perform at work. Finding solutions is increasingly difficult the more you worry about money. Together, we'll end this cycle.

Techniques for Taking Back Control

Gather all of your financial data in one location to start creating a clear financial snapshot. This comprises receipts, bills, debts, and sources of revenue. Your strategy will be built on an accurate picture of your financial status.

1. Set attainable financial objectives that are clear and realistic. Having specific goals can

inspire and direct you, whether they be for vacation savings, credit card debt repayment, or emergency fund building.

2. Create a Budget: Your road map to financial security is a well-structured budget. We'll walk you through the process of making a budget that provides for both your necessities and your ambitions and aspirations.

3. Emergency reserve: One of the most important steps in easing financial strain is to create an emergency reserve. We'll go through how to build one and why it should be your backup plan for money.

4. Debt Management: If managing your debt is causing you worry, we'll look at several

techniques for doing so. Take charge of your financial commitments now.

5. Seek Professional Assistance: If you're feeling overwhelmed, don't be afraid to speak with financial experts or counselors. They may provide professional advice catered to your unique scenario.

Self-care is important since financial stress may negatively impact both your physical and emotional well-being. We'll talk about how to take care of yourself to reduce stress and have a good outlook.

Conclusion

It takes time to get rid of financial stress, but if you use the techniques in this chapter and are dedicated to taking back control, you can start along the path to financial stability and serenity. Keep in mind that you are not doing this task alone and that each step you take will bring you one step closer to a future free from financial worry. We will continue to build upon these foundations in the next chapters as we direct you toward your road to financial success.

Chapter 3

Financial Management Expertise

Setting financial goals and taking charge of your financial situation have been explored in earlier chapters. It's time to learn more about one of the cornerstones of achieving financial success: effective money management. Consider this chapter your manual for creating a budget that fits your particular lifestyle and learning practical strategies for adhering to your financial plan.

Making Your Budget

Although making a budget may seem tedious or constrictive to some, it is the basis for financial stability and expansion. A well-designed budget should ensure that you utilize your resources effectively to meet your financial objectives while still living life to the fullest. It shouldn't involve denying yourself the things you like.

Step 1: Understand Your Financial Environment

Get a thorough awareness of your financial condition to start. Gather all of your pay stubs, bank statements, financial statements, and any pertinent paperwork. Determine your entire income, taking into account your main employment, any side jobs, and any other sources of money.

List all of your costs next. Sort them into variable costs like eating out, entertainment, and hobbies, as well as fixed costs like rent or a mortgage, utilities, and insurance. Don't forget to budget for erratic charges like maintenance fees or yearly subscriptions.

Set specific financial goals in step two.

Establish your financial objectives before delving into the technical details of your budget. What do you want to accomplish in the near and long term? Your objectives will guide your budgeting choices, whether they are putting up an emergency fund, paying off debt, or preparing for a dream trip.

Step 3: Budget Your Money

Allocate your revenue among the different spending categories keeping in mind your objectives. Place a higher priority on necessities like food, utilities, shelter, and debt repayment. Then, set aside some money for savings and investments to help you achieve your financial goals. Finally, set aside a manageable sum for discretionary spending so you may enjoy life guilt-free.

How to Maintain Your Financial Plan

1. Making a budget is simple; keeping it up might be difficult. The secret to success is adopting tried-and-true methods and developing productive routines. The following tactics can assist you in sticking to your financial plan:

2. Automate Savings: As soon as your paycheck arrives, set up automated transfers to your savings and investing accounts. This guarantees that you are continually pursuing your objectives.

3. Track Your Spending: Use spreadsheets for budgeting tools to keep tabs on your spending in real-time. You can modify your spending habits if you are aware of where your money is going.

4. Create Accountability: Tell a family member or trusted friend about your financial objectives so they can assist you in staying on track. Talking about your accomplishments might inspire you.

5. Practice Delayed Gratification: Allow yourself a "cooling-off" time before making non-essential purchases. After a few days, if you still want it, go ahead, but you'll typically discover that the need fades.

6. Celebrate Your Small Successes: Recognize and Enjoy Your Successes Along the Way. Recognizing your accomplishments keeps you motivated, whether it's paying off a credit card or reaching a savings goal.

7. Review and Adjust Your Budget Frequently: Because life is dynamic, your budget should too. To keep on track, review your budget often and make any modifications.

Developing a financial plan that enables you to live the life you want is an important part of mastering money management. In the chapters that follow, we'll look at other methods for assisting you in realizing your financial goals. Keep in mind that each financial path is unique, and you can make each step toward financial happiness count with the correct tools and mentality.

Section 2

Creating Wealth from Income

Your money is your most valuable resource as you strive for financial success. generating the most of your earnings is more important than just generating money. We'll go into tactics in this chapter that will enable you to take charge of your earning potential.

Activating the Negotiation Process

Do you often question if you are being paid what you are worth? Whether you're negotiating pay in a new job or asking for a raise in your current one, negotiation is a great tool for increasing your income. We'll look at tried-and-true bargaining strategies that may help you get a bigger paycheck and improve your financial future.

Creating Opportunities for Income

Your 9 to 5 work is not the only factor that determines your financial success. We'll find several ways for you to make money apart from your normal job. You'll discover how to diversify your income sources and make your money work for you, from side jobs and freelancing to investment income.

This chapter aims to provide you with the information and abilities you need to turn your income into riches. You'll have a thorough grasp of how to increase your earning potential and lay the groundwork for long-term financial stability by the time you finish reading this section.

Chapter 4

Maximizing Your Earning Potential

The key to financial success in today's fast-paced world isn't only careful budgeting and saving; it's also about maximizing your earning potential. This chapter serves as your key to unlocking the techniques that will enable you to demand the pay you deserve and open doors to significant financial gain.

A Negotiation's Art

Anyone who wants to increase their income must learn how to negotiate. Your capacity to bargain successfully may have a big influence on your financial situation, whether you're wrangling over freelancing fees, discussing a starting pay for new employment, or negotiating a raise at your existing work.

Recognizing Your Value

It's essential to know your genuine market value before engaging in any negotiations. Examine your abilities and experience, research industry compensation norms, and take into account your organization's particular contributions. This information will act as your compass throughout negotiations, preventing you from accepting less than you are entitled to.

The Art of Negotiation

An organized approach to bargaining is essential for success:

1. Planning: Compile information, practice talking points, and foresee potential objections.

Introduction: Make a strong opening statement, demonstrate curiosity, and establish a favorable tone.

2. Exploration: Pay close attention, probe the other person's viewpoint, and ask questions.

3. Presentation: Explain your value, make your argument, and provide proof to back up your assertions.

4. When haggling, be adaptable but don't give up too early. Seek a solution that will benefit all parties.

5. Agreement: Once the details are worked out, put everything in writing.

Going Above and Beyond Salary

6. The negotiation process goes beyond salary. Think about haggling for extra advantages like:
Bonuses and commissions: Performance-based rewards may substantially increase your income.

8. Flexible Work Schedules: Consider choices like remote employment, adjustable working hours, or shorter work weeks.

9. Professional Development: Bargain for chances to further your education or expand your skills.

10. Equity and Stock Options: Equity may be a useful asset in new or existing businesses.

11. Extra perks: Transportation stipends, fitness initiatives, and health perks may add up.

Making Provisions for Financial Development

Negotiations may result in short-term revenue increases, but prospects for long-term financial success need proactive thinking and careful preparation.

Enterprise-related Activities

Think about starting a side hustle or a small company that is in line with your interests and qualifications. The gig economy provides a variety of options for making money off of your skills and hobbies, from consulting and freelancing to online businesses.

Investment Techniques

By making prudent investments, diversify your sources of income. Examine several investing options, including stocks, bonds, properties, and retirement accounts. To create a balanced portfolio, be aware of your risk tolerance and seek the advice of financial professionals.

Continuous Education

By continuing to study, you are investing in yourself. Learning new abilities and information may lead to better-paying jobs and professional development. Online seminars, certificates, and courses are easier to obtain than ever.

Mentoring and networking

Create a robust professional network and look for mentors who can provide advice and assistance. Through networking, one may find partnerships, career leads, and insightful information about market trends.

Making Use of Technology

Utilize technology to your advantage to raise your earning potential. Freelancing websites and platforms like LinkedIn link professionals with opportunities throughout the globe.

Your Potential for Earning Waits

You may significantly increase your earning potential by developing your bargaining skills and aggressively looking for ways to improve your financial situation. Keep in mind that your revenue might change and increase as you do. You now have the means to make sure that your financial future is as bright as your goals thanks to the tactics described in this chapter.

Chapter 5

Investment Magic: Growing Your Money

The skill of investing is one of the most effective weapons at your disposal in the quest for monetary success and the fulfillment of your aspirations. In this chapter, we'll explain how to use wise investing techniques to enhance your financial resources. But let's address two essential issues first: demystifying investing and mastering risk management before we go into the realm of investments.

Investments: Dispelling Myths

Investments may sometimes seem to be a mysterious realm wrapped in confusing terminology and unpredictability. However, it's important to realize that investing is not a field exclusive to money geniuses. You may confidently go along this realistic route to money growth.

We'll dissect investing ideas, beginning with the basics. We'll provide a straightforward explanation of how stocks, bonds, real estate, and other investment instruments operate. You will have the information necessary to make knowledgeable investing selections that are suited to your financial objectives after this chapter.

Risk control: Your protector in the world of investing

Although investing entails risks by nature, it is not a game of luck. This game requires careful risk management and planning. We'll go through how to determine your risk tolerance and develop a tailored investing plan that fits your comfort zone. By learning to differentiate between various risk kinds, from market volatility to individual investment hazards, you'll be able to make decisions that fit your financial strategy.

We'll also explore the vital idea of diversity. Consider it as practicing the skill of spreading your financial risks. Your defense against unanticipated financial storms is diversifying your investments. You'll learn how to diversify your holdings across a range of asset types and sectors to reduce risk and maximize profits.

Your Diversified Investment Portfolio: Putting It Together

This chapter's last section will walk you through the stages involved in creating a diverse investment portfolio in practice. To assist you in achieving the correct balance between stability and growth, we'll examine asset allocation options. You will learn about the advantages of long-term investment and how patience may be your most effective asset in building money.

You'll leave this chapter with the information and self-assurance needed to join the world of investing thanks to examples from real-world situations and professional counsel. Possessing a thorough grasp of investments and a calculated approach to risk management can pave the way for your financial success.

Never forget that investing is a well-planned path toward realizing your financial goals rather than a quick fix for success. So let's start this journey, debunk the world of investing, and learn the real secrets of increasing your money for a better financial future.

Section 3

Blueprint for a Secure Future

"Imagine yourself enjoying your favorite beverage on a tranquil veranda on a fresh, bright morning. Your well-earned retirement has left behind the stresses of your regular job and replaced them with tranquility. You can have the moment you've been longing for right now.

We will explore the art of making retirement goals a reality in this chapter. We'll work with you to picture your dream retirement, whether it involves globe travel, charitable work, or just spending time with loved ones. However, it goes beyond just dreaming. To make sure that your retirement is not just a dream but a well-planned, financially secure chapter of your life, we will walk you through specific solutions.

We'll examine several retirement products, such as 401(k)s and IRAs, and decipher the financial lingo used to describe them. To create a nest egg that will support your aspirations, you'll learn how to optimize your contributions and establish reasonable savings objectives.

Therefore, you're at the perfect spot if you've ever pondered how to turn your retirement goals into a reality, concerned about running out of money, or just want to make sure your golden years are golden. Let's translate these aspirations into a plan for a safe and happy future.

This chapter lays the groundwork for an in-depth investigation of retirement planning by encouraging readers to picture their perfect retirement and assuring them that they can make it happen with the appropriate tactics.

Chapter 6

Dreams for Retirement

Retirement stands out as a destination when you set out on your route to financial happiness. Retirement is a culmination of your hard work, ambitions, and objectives, not merely a stage in life. We'll look at the process of creating and achieving your retirement goals in this chapter. We'll look into tactics that may help you realize your ambitions as well as ensure a pleasant retirement.

The Influence of Vision

Let's start with a potent exercise: visualization, before we get into the actual parts of retirement planning. For a little minute, close your eyes and visualize your dream retirement. Do you notice anything? Spending more time with your grandkids or maybe waking up to the tranquil sound of waves lapping on a beach. Setting the coordinates on your financial GPS by visualizing your retirement offers you a specific destination to aim toward.

Consider these questions as you go through this exercise:

- Where do you wish to reside after you retire?
- What will you do to pass the time?

- How do you see your relationships and social life developing?
- What kind of legacy do you want to leave for the world or your loved ones?

You'll get motivation and clarity by creating a detailed image of your retirement. You'll be motivated to take the required actions to make this vision a reality.

A Comfortable Retirement: Strategies

Your retirement aspirations may become a reality with the right planning, not just wishful thinking. Let's look at some crucial tactics to guarantee a pleasant retirement:

1. Start Early: When it comes to retirement savings, time is your biggest ally. The sooner you start investing and saving, the more

compound interest will increase your money.

2. Set Specific Goals: Clearly state what you want your retirement to look like. How much money are you going to need to keep living the way you want to? Making a realistic strategy is made easier when you are aware of your goal.

3. Spread your assets across several asset classes to reduce risk by diversifying your investments. Your retirement nest egg might be protected from market volatility with a well-balanced portfolio.

4. Contribute as much as possible to retirement accounts, such as 401(k)s, IRAs,

or other plans offered in your nation. Use employer matches if they are offered.

5. Life is full of surprises, so examine and tweak your retirement strategy as necessary. Modifications can be necessary if your objectives, spending, or income change.

6. Healthcare Planning: Take retirement healthcare expenses into account. To prevent unforeseen costs, you should consider Medicare or other health insurance choices.

7. Take into account prospective sources of retirement income, including pensions, Social Security, and, if desired, part-time employment.

8. Consult a financial advisor: A specialist can assist you in developing a personalized retirement strategy, maximizing your savings, and navigating complex retirement rules.

We'll examine each of these tactics in more detail in the pages that follow, offering you helpful advice and insights to help you realize your retirement goals.

Recall that retirement isn't the conclusion of the road; rather, it's the start of a brand-new exciting chapter in your life. You can make sure that it's a chapter filled with happiness, contentment, and financial stability with careful preparation and effort.

Let's begin, one step at a time, to make your retirement fantasies a reality.

Chapter 7

Family Security and Legacies

Making Sure Your Values Survive and Your Loved Ones Are Successful

The numerous components of financial success have been covered in the earlier chapters, from learning the fine art of budgeting to navigating the complexities of investing. We are about to enter a chapter that speaks directly to many people's motivations: ensuring the welfare of our family and leaving a lasting legacy.

The Meaning of Legacies

A tribute to your beliefs, convictions, and the influence you've had on the lives of people you love dear, your legacy is more than simply a cash gift. As we go through this chapter, we'll think about ways to protect the future of your family and create an inheritance plan that aligns with your values.

Taking Financial Security for Your Family's Future

Your family's financial stability is important, therefore making an estate plan carefully is essential. By dividing the process down into simple phases, we'll be able to navigate the tricky seas of estate planning in these pages. This chapter will provide you the direction you need whether you're just beginning to think about these issues or already have a strategy that needs to be improved.

Beyond Financial Legacies

We'll discuss the practical parts of estate planning, but we'll also look at the emotional and intellectual components of leaving a legacy. What principles do you want your successors to carry on? What tales and teachings ought they to pass on? We'll talk about how to pass down your knowledge and ideals to the generations who will come after you since your legacy goes well beyond monetary prosperity.

Making a Will That Reflects Your Values

When it comes to estate planning, one size does not fit all. Your strategy should be an accurate reflection of your circumstances, aspirations, and values. We'll guide you through the process of drafting an estate plan that safeguards your financial resources, reduces tax obligations, and makes sure that money is transferred to your heirs without difficulty. We'll also go through the many instruments you have available, such as wills trusts, and charitable giving plans.

The Knowledge Legacy

Remember as we close up this chapter that your legacy isn't only about the money you leave behind. Your loved ones will be very grateful for the information and experience you've acquired on your financial path. They may be empowered to make wise financial choices and carry on the values of financial success you've adopted by hearing about your experiences and ideas.

We'll set out on a journey in the pages that follow to safeguard your family's future and leave a lasting legacy. Let's get started on estate planning so you may take proactive measures to make sure your loved ones are successful and your values are upheld.

Section 4

Thriving While Traveling

It's simple to lose focus on what's important in the case of financial success. The confluence of money and well-being, which is the location of genuine prosperity, is what this chapter serves as your compass.

Balancing Well-Being and Wealth

Financial success is a means to a goal—a full life—rather than an end in and of itself. We go deeply into the art of balancing, assisting you in finding the ideal balance between building money and living an experience- and content-rich life. Learn how to enjoy the now while making preparations for the future.

Unlocking the Giving Power

Being generous may have a positive impact on others and you. We investigate the positive effects of charitable giving and serving the community. Learn how combining your sense of purpose with your financial success may increase the satisfaction you feel from your accomplishments.

Developing Mental Wealth and Resilience

Financial difficulties are a necessary part of life. In this part, we provide you with the techniques and skills you need to overcome challenges and emerge stronger than before. You'll learn how to manage stress, worry, and failures gracefully and examine the significance of mental toughness in your financial path.

The Experiment with Money

Finally, we extend our perspective and set off on a voyage that is unconstrained by money. While having money is important for living a happy life, it is not the only indicator of our value. We'll work with you to clarify your idea of what a fulfilling life looks like and examine how your material success fits into that bigger picture.

You will have the information and skills necessary to succeed financially as well as the freedom to lead a life that is genuinely wealthy in all respects by the time you finish this chapter. Your path to financial joy involves more than simply building riches; it also entails enlarging your spirit, discovering your purpose, and appreciating each step along the route.

Chapter 8

Wealthy Mindfulness

It's easy to get solely focused on the figures, the investments, and the bottom line while pursuing financial success. However, as you've read through this book, you've seen that riches are much more than just money. The quality of your life, your feeling of purpose, and your general well-being are all parts of true prosperity. This chapter focuses on the idea of conscious wealth, which is the skill of juggling your material success with your overall well-being.

The View of Holistic Wealth

It's crucial to change your viewpoint to fully understand the meaning of mindful wealth. Wealth should be seen as a jewel with several facets, each of which represents a distinct area of your life. These aspects consist of:

1. Financial Stability

Undoubtedly, one of the most important aspects of wealth is financial stability. It entails prudent money management, creating and accomplishing financial objectives, and planning for the future. You've learned a variety of techniques to improve your financial situation throughout this book.

2. Physical Fitness

Financial affluence may become dull without excellent health. Your quality of life is strongly impacted by your physical health. Consistent exercise, a healthy diet, and enough sleep are all crucial components of conscious wealth.

3. Mood and Mental Health

Your emotional and mental well-being are equally important. The advantages of financial success might be diminished by stress, worry, and bad emotions. We'll look into techniques for controlling stress and creating emotional toughness.

4. Relationships

Relationships should be strengthened by wealth rather than strained. A happy life depends on having strong relationships with friends, family, and other loved ones. Learn how to maintain these relationships while you progress financially.

5. Personal Development and Contentment
Constant personal development and following your interests are essential components of conscious wealth. We'll look at how achieving financial success may contribute to personal development and satisfaction.

The Equation for Mindful Wealth

A tailored strategy is needed to balance these aspects of conscious wealth. Think about this equation:

Financial success, good physical and mental health, happiness in relationships, and personal development all contribute to mindful wealth.

You can see that achieving financial success is just one part of the puzzle. Harmony between each of these components is necessary for mindful riches. Realizing that these aspects of your life should be enhanced rather than burdened by your financial path is important.

Mindfulness Techniques for Wellness

We'll go into useful mindful techniques to assist you in achieving this balance in the parts of this chapter that follow. We'll discuss ways to reduce stress, tactics for improving your physical and mental health, and methods for fostering relationships and personal development while advancing your financial success.

Keep in mind that mindful wealth is a lifetime process rather than a goal. It involves matching your financial decisions to your moral principles to use your riches as a tool for living a richer, more satisfying life. Let's start this journey mindfully by adopting a holistic approach to prosperity and enjoying the life-affirming harmony it delivers.

Chapter 9

The Trip Goes On

Your financial path is no different from life in that it is a twisting road. The hurdles and disappointments that might inevitably arise on the road to financial achievement are discussed in Chapter 9. But keep in mind that your path is ultimately defined by how you overcome these challenges.

Accepting Failures

Failures in business are inevitable in life. Setbacks are the humps in the path that put our commitment to the test, whether it's an unanticipated medical expenditure, a job loss, or a market slump. In this part, we'll look at ways to survive these storms while still emerging from them stronger.

1. The Mindset of Resilience
First, we work on developing a resilient attitude. Knowing that obstacles are just transitory and that you have the power to overcome them is key. We'll go deeply into mental techniques that might keep you calm and on task when faced with financial difficulty.

2. Emergency Preparedness
Having a sizable emergency fund is one of the best strategies for dealing with setbacks. We'll go through how to create and keep up an emergency fund that may serve as a safety net for money in trying times.

Long-Term Financial Success Techniques

Although obstacles are a part of the path, long-term financial success is the ultimate objective. We'll learn tactics in this part that will not only help you bounce back from failures but also get you closer to your financial goals.

3. Reviewing Objectives

We may need to reassess our financial objectives in response to setbacks. To make sure that your objectives continue to be in line with your changing priorities, we'll lead you through a process of reflection.

4. Risk reduction and diversification

Long-term financial success depends on diversifying your assets and controlling risk. We'll look at cutting-edge tactics to safeguard and expand your money even in unstable economic conditions.

5. Creating Resilient Behaviors
Consistent behaviors are the foundation of long-term success. We'll talk about developing sound financial practices that will serve you well as you work toward financial security.

Conclusion

We admit in Chapter 9 that achieving financial success isn't always easy. But what will make you stand out on your trip are the abilities and tactics you pick up through these trying times. You may thrive along the trip by accepting failures and putting long-term success methods into practice. So let's work through these difficulties together while maintaining an eye on the promise of financial security.

Chapter 10

Your Financial Success Roadmap

In the earlier chapters, we looked at the many aspects of financial success, digging into tactics, perceptions, and information to help you on your path. It's time to put everything together and create your financial success road plan.

Setting Goals for Financial Success

Let's review your goals before we go out on the adventure to design your plan. What exactly do you mean by "financial bliss"? Is it having the freedom to visit any country? giving your kids a high-quality education?

retiring comfortably and early? Or maybe it's all of the aforementioned.

Your definition of financial joy serves as the North Star for all of your financial choices. It's about living the life you want to live, not simply the numbers on a spreadsheet. Consider your future for a minute, savoring the emotions, encounters, and successes connected to your financial objectives.

The Three Foundations of Your Map

Clarity, Strategy, and Action are the three sturdily built pillars that support your financial success roadmap.

First pillar: Clarity

The power lies in clarity. Get a clear knowledge of your present financial condition to start. You will be guided through:

- Evaluating your earnings, outgoings, possessions, and debts.
- Recognizing your financial assets and liabilities.
- Defining your immediate and long-term objectives.

You can only plot a route to where you want to go once you are aware of where you are.

Component 2: Strategy

Clarity leads to strategy. We'll assist you:

- Create a budget that is specific to your objectives.
- Investigate investing opportunities that meet your risk appetite.
- If required, develop a debt-reduction strategy.
- Create plans to increase your revenue.

A well-designed plan serves as a compass, guiding your financial choices in the direction you want to go.

Step 3: Take action

Although having a plan is important, without taking action, they are just blueprints. This section will go particularly deeply into:

- How to organize and carry out your financial objectives.
- Hints for maintaining self-control and inspiration along the road.

Techniques for adjusting to life's ups and downs while maintaining focus on your financial nirvana.

Your Journey, Your Roadmap

Keep in mind that your financial success roadmap does not apply to everyone. It is made just for your individual needs, goals, and objectives. You're in control, and this route map is your reliable roadside assistance.

You'll find useful activities, worksheets, and examples from real life throughout this chapter to help you create your roadmap. By putting everything you've learned in this book into practice, you may start your road to financial happiness.

As we wrap off this chapter and your reading of this book, know that you have the information, resources, and motivation you need to find financial success. Even if the route may include curves and turns, you are well-prepared for the journey since you have your guidebook in hand.

Therefore, let's get started creating your financial success roadmap. It's time to start achieving your goals, one deliberate step at a time. Welcome to a time where achieving financial success is possible and your goals become your legacy.

Resources and Tools Appendix

Sincere congratulations on starting your path to financial success! We have put together a collection of priceless materials, informative worksheets, and useful tools that will function as your compass on your journey to further empower you. These tools are intended to support you in taking decisive action, selecting wisely, and continuously improving your financial plan.

1. Reading that is advised:

Discover more about personal finance with our hand-picked collection of books written by famous financial professionals. These books address a broad variety of subjects, including wealth-building strategies, investing, and budgeting. Through these smart books, you may increase your knowledge and improve your financial skills.

2. Digital Worksheets:

Our selection of interactive worksheets is designed to make challenging financial chores simple. These user-friendly templates can help you crunch the numbers and get a clear view of your financial situation, whether you're making a budget, keeping track of your spending, or establishing savings goals.

3. Investment Resources

We have a series of helpful resources offered for people who are keen to investigate investing options. You can analyze risk, predict returns, and make wise investment choices with the aid of these calculators and investing guidelines. Growing your money properly is the first step on your path to financial joy, and these tools will be your dependable allies.

4. Platforms for online financial planning:

Learn about internet tools and software that help make your financial planning process more efficient. These digital tools, which range from retirement calculators to budgeting applications, make it easy and precise to manage your money. We've done our homework and created a list of platforms that are suitable for your budget.

5. Financial advisors' contact details are as follows:

We've included contact details for licensed financial advisers in your region should you want individualized advice on your financial path. These experts may provide you with individualized guidance and tactics to hasten the achievement of your financial objectives.

6. Online Community Exclusive:

Join our exclusive online group of like-minded people who are also seeking financial happiness. Share your insights, get suggestions, and be inspired by other readers who have taken similar adventures.

Keep in mind that this Appendix is there to help you while you are through a financial shift. Watch as you steadily get closer to opening the door to your financial happiness by making good use of this information and tools, customizing them to your situation.

I hope your future is prosperous and rewarding!

(George T. Y.)

www.ingramcontent.com/pod-product-compliance
Lightning Source LLC
Chambersburg PA
CBHW062355290526
45794CB00005B/2230